How Did We Find Out About OUTER SPACE?

ISAAC ASIMOV is a distinguished scientist as well as America's foremost writer on science for both adults and young readers. Born in Russia, Mr. Asimov came to this country with his parents at the age of three, and grew up in Brooklyn. He has written over two hundred books, and his instincts for probing the unknown and his warm understanding of human nature draw millions of readers—young and old—to his writings.

DAVID WOOL is a well-known commercial artist and industrial designer. His interests range from raising cats to studying history and archaeology.

How Did We Find Out About OUTER SPACE?

Isaac Asimov

Illustrated by David Wool

Isaac Asimov

AVON BOOKS
A division of
The Hearst Corporation
959 Eighth Avenue
New York, New York 10019

Published by arrangement with Walker and Company
Library of Congress Catalog Card Number: 76-57064
ISBN: 0-380-53413-4

Cover Illustration and Design by Art–So–Fine Studios

First Camelot Printing, February, 1981

CAMELOT TRADEMARK REG. U.S. PAT. OFF. AND IN
OTHER COUNTRIES, MARCA REGISTRADA, HECHO EN U.S.A.

Printed in the U.S.A.

10 9 8 7 6 5 4 3 2 1

To my warm friends
Barbara and Ben Bova

Contents

1 FLYING 9

2 VACUUM 19

3 ROCKETS 29

4 LIQUID-FUEL ROCKETS 39

5 SATELLITES AND SPACESHIPS 49

INDEX 61

1 Flying

PEOPLE MOVE by walking, running, hopping, skipping, jumping, crawling, swimming, or turning cartwheels. No matter what they do, though, their bodies touch the ground at almost all times. If a person jumps and moves through the air, that lasts only a few seconds, and then he or she is down again on the ground.

This is not true of all animals. Birds, bats, and insects can all fly. Their wings beat against the air. While they fly, the air holds them up as the ground holds us up.

There seems to be such freedom in flying. You don't have to climb over rocks and hills, or wade across rivers, or slog through mud. You just move through the clear air in any direction you want to go. There have been times, I am sure, when you wished you could flap your arms and take off like a bird.

In ancient times people also wished they could fly and made up stories in which flying was possible. They told about carpets that could fly if you only

ICARUS

knew the right magic word that would start them off. They told of winged horses that could carry their riders swiftly through the air.

The most famous ancient story about flying was made up by the ancient Greeks over 2,500 years ago. They told of a clever inventor, Daedalus *(DED-uh-lus)*, who, with his son, Icarus (*IK-uh-rus*), was imprisoned on an island near Crete. Daedalus had no boat, so in order to escape from the island he made wings for himself and his son. He built a light wooden framework, covered it with wax, and stuck feathers into the wax. By flapping these wings he could rise in the air and fly. Together, he and Icarus flew away. Daedalus reached Sicily about 500 miles away, but Icarus, in the joy of flying, soared too high. Approaching the sun, he found the heat melting the wax. The feathers on his wings were loosened, fell off, and Icarus fell to his death.

The story is an impossible one, of course. Wings alone can't make you fly, even when they have feathers on them. What counts are the muscles used to flap the wings strongly enough to lift the body into the air. The heavier an animal, the stronger the muscles must be to allow it to fly. With the kind of muscles animals have, the heaviest any flying animal can be is about 50 pounds.

No human being can lift his weight by using his or her muscles to flap wings. It's even more impossible for a horse to do so.

But then, perhaps a person can use many birds hitched to some sort of chariot. Each bird would carry just a tiny bit of weight in addition to its own. In the

CHARIOT DRAWN BY GEESE

1630s, an English writer, Francis Godwin, wrote a story called *Man in the Moone*. He told of an explorer who hitched many great geese to a chariot. The geese flew up in the air, lifted the chariot with the man in it, and carried him so high as to bring him to the moon. No one, however, has ever really tried to hitch many birds to a chariot.

About a century and a half after Godwin wrote his book human beings did find a way to get off the surface of the earth. It wasn't by magic or by flapping their arms, however. It was by floating.

A Frenchman, Joseph Montgolfier (*mone-gole-FYAY*), and his younger brother, Jacques, noticed that the smoke from fires rises and lifts light things with it. It seemed that hot air is lighter (that is, *less dense*) than cold air. That means that hot air will

J. MONTGOLFIER'S BALLOON
1783

move upward through cold air, just as a piece of wood will move upward through water.

On June 5, 1783, in the marketplace of their hometown, the brothers filled a large linen bag with hot air. The hot air rose, carrying the bag upward too, and drifted for a mile and a half in ten minutes. By then the hot air had cooled down, and this first *balloon* could fly no more.

In November the brothers demonstrated a hot-air balloon in Paris. A crowd of 300,000 people watched as the balloon rose. This time it floated six miles.

A very light gas, hydrogen (*HIGH-droh-jen*), had just been discovered. It is much less dense than hot air. In fact, it is the least dense gas known. A French scientist, Jacques Charles (*SHAHRL*), suggested that balloons be filled with hydrogen.

This was done, and hydrogen-filled balloons lifted gondolas with human beings in them up into the sky. In the early 1800s many people went ballooning. For the first time people could rise miles into the air.

Balloons can only drift with the wind. Suppose, though, you place some kind of engine in the gondola that will turn a propeller. The rapidly turning propeller would drive the balloon through the air in any direction, just as a propeller on a ship drives it through the water. A balloon driven by a propeller would be a *dirigible*; that is, a balloon that could be *directed*.

The first dirigible was constructed by a German, Count Ferdinand von Zeppelin (*TSEP-ih-lin*). He put the balloon into a long cigar-shaped case of the light metal aluminum (*uh-LOO-mih-num*) so it would cut through the air more easily. On July 2, 1900, the first dirigible moved through the air. People could now fly in any direction they pleased.

For over 40 years, dirigibles were made bigger and better, but the hydrogen used to fill them was dangerous. Hydrogen is inflammable and can explode.

COUNT FERDINAND VON ZEPPELIN
1838-1917

Another light gas, helium (*HEE-lee-um*), could be used instead. It doesn't lift quite as well as hydrogen does, but helium never catches fire. Even so, dirigibles didn't move very quickly, and they weren't very strong. They broke up easily in storms.

Of course, some things can move through the air even when they are too dense to float. A kite is denser than air, but it floats because it presents a large surface to the air. It catches even light winds and can be held up by them. What if kites were built large enough to carry a man?

Boatlike objects were built of very light wood, and flat pieces of wood (*wings*) were attached in order to catch more of the air. Such *gliders* could be made big enough to carry a man. If they were launched into the air from a height, they could stay in the air quite a while, catching the wind and updrafts. In the 1890s the use of gliders became quite popular.

Gliders, like balloons, could only go where the wind took them. Could an engine be mounted on a glider to turn a propeller, as von Zeppelin had mounted one on a balloon?

In Dayton, Ohio, two American bicycle manufacturers, Orville Wright and his brother, Wilbur, decided to try to do this. They built gliders that would take full advantage of the wind, and motors that were as light as possible.

On December 17, 1903, at Kitty Hawk, North Carolina, Orville Wright was carried through the air by a powered glider. It was the first *airplane*. It only stayed in the air for about a minute, and it only traveled 850 feet, but it showed it could be done.

Airplanes were made bigger. They had better engines so they moved faster. The faster an airplane moves, the more the air lifts the wings and the heavier the plane can be. In 1908 Orville Wright remained in the air for an hour. In 1909 an airplane was flown across the English Channel. During World War I airplanes zoomed and shot at each other. In 1927 the American aviator Charles A. Lindbergh flew across the Atlantic from New York to Paris all by himself in a plane. It took him 33 hours.

ORVILLE WRIGHT AT CONTROLS
Dec. 17, 1903, Kitty Hawk

Nowadays airplanes have become so big they can carry hundreds of people. Some planes can move at a speed of 1,000 miles an hour or more, and they can cross the Atlantic in 3 hours.

Airplanes have completely replaced dirigibles, but ordinary balloons are still used to study the air high above the surface of the earth. Special balloons made of light, thin plastic can rise nearly 30 miles above the surface of the earth.

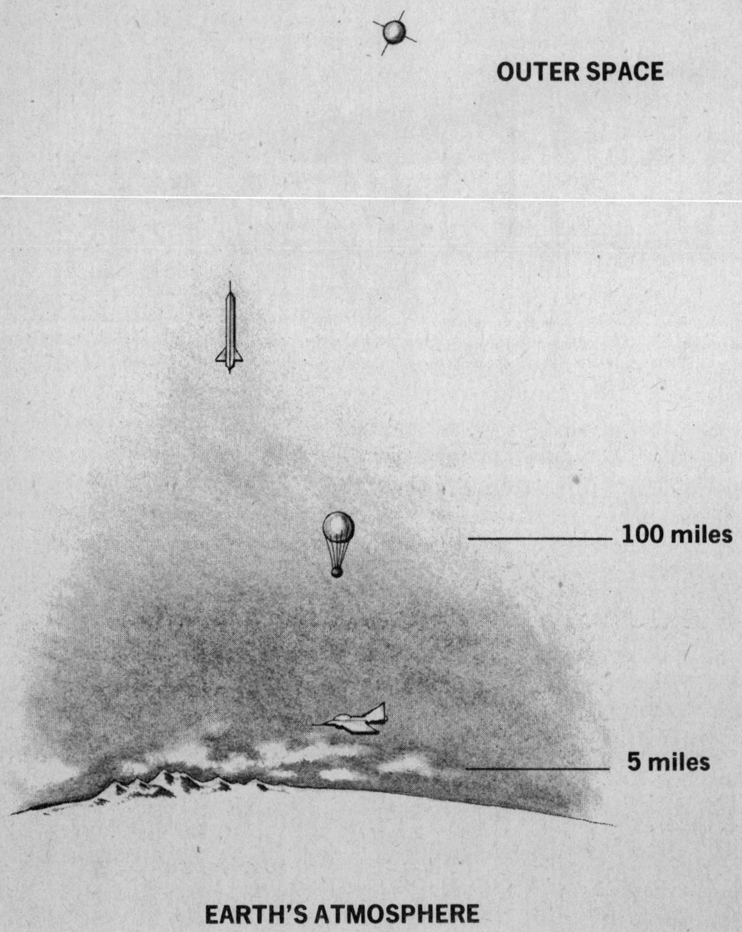

OUTER SPACE

100 miles

5 miles

EARTH'S ATMOSPHERE

2 Vacuum

Now that we have have balloons and airplanes that can carry people miles into the air, why don't we keep on rising higher and higher, as the man in Godwin's story did, until we reach the moon?

The trouble is that balloons and ordinary airplanes depend on air. Balloons float on air. Speeding airplanes are held up by air. Then, too, airplanes need a gas called oxygen (*OK-sih-jen*), which is present in air, to combine with the fuel they use and keep their engines going.

The question, then, is how high up does the air go?

The ancients took it for granted that the air just stretched upward indefinitely, right up to the moon and all the other objects in the sky. The people who wrote stories about going to the moon seemed to think it was no harder and took no longer to cross the ocean of air from the earth to the moon than it was to cross the ocean of water from Europe to America.

Just a few years after Godwin had written his

book, however, new discoveries changed our attitude toward air.

In 1643 an Italian scientist, Evangelista Torricelli (*tor-rih-CHEL-lee*), took a four-foot length of glass tubing that was open at one end and filled it with mercury. Torricelli then stoppered the open end and upended the tube into a basin of mercury. He then unstoppered it.

You might think all the mercury would pour out, but only part did. The pressure of the air pushing against the surface of the mercury in the basin held up a column of mercury 30 inches high in the tube. Torricelli had devised the first *barometer* (*buh-ROM-uh-ter*), and it could be used to measure changes in air pressure.

Imagine a column of air an inch wide stretching upward a certain distance. How high must that column of air be to weigh as much as a column of mercury an inch wide and 30 inches high? A given amount of mercury weighs 10,500 times as much as the same amount of the air. The column of air must be 10,500 times as high as the mercury to weigh as much. That means that the air must be five miles high.

Actually, the air is higher than that. The lower part of the air, near the earth's surface, is pushed together or *compressed* by the weight of the upper parts. The air near the surface is therefore denser than the air higher up.

In fact, the higher you go, the thinner and less dense the air gets. The air takes up more and more room the thinner it gets. This means that the air

EVANGELISTA TORRICELLI AND THE FIRST BAROMETER

stretches up much more than five miles from the earth's surface. There is some air even a hundred miles above the surface.

As the air gets thinner, however, it becomes less and less useful. Six miles up the air is already too thin to breathe. Thirty miles up the air is too thin to float a balloon or support an airplane. A hundred miles up the air is so thin it can hardly be detected.

Yet even a hundred miles is hardly any distance at all when it comes to reaching the moon. The moon is

240,000 miles from the earth. Almost all that distance, then, has no air at all. It is a "vacuum" (*VAK-you-um*), which is from a Latin word meaning "empty."

A vacuum is found almost everywhere in the universe. You will find air very close to a planet, but sometimes not even then. There is no air on the moon, for instance. The vacuum comes right down to its surface.

We might call the vacuum that exists beyond the atmosphere *outer space*. We can say, therefore, that Torricelli was the discoverer of outer space. He was the first person to show that the air does not go up to the sky, that it is only present close to the earth's surface.

This means that no one can travel to the moon as Godwin's hero did. Even if large geese could pull a chariot, they couldn't fly in a vacuum. They couldn't even breathe in a vacuum, nor could a man. No balloon could float upward into a vacuum. No airplane could fly in a vacuum.

Even after people had learned to fly in balloons, dirigibles, gliders, and airplanes, they could not rise more than a few miles above the surface of the planet.

How can people reach the moon, then? Is there any way something can be made to move through a vacuum?

One way is to throw something. If you throw a ball into the air, it flies upward because of the push given it by your muscles. The air has nothing to do with it. In fact, the air resists the motion and makes the ball move more slowly than it would if you threw it up into a vacuum.

Of course, a ball doesn't move very high. The earth's gravity keeps pulling at it and slowing it down. Eventually, its upward motion slows to nothing. For an instant the ball hangs motionless in the air, and then it starts falling.

The harder you throw the ball, the faster it moves to begin with. The faster it moves, the longer it takes the gravitational pull to slow it down and the higher it goes before it starts falling again.

Suppose you throw a ball harder and harder and watch it go higher and higher before it falls down. Will it always eventually fall down no matter how hard you throw it? Will it always come down no matter how fast it goes upward to begin with?

If earth's gravitational pull stayed just as strong as it is here on the surface no matter how high you went, then the ball would *always* eventually come down, no matter how hard you threw it. However, as it happens, earth's gravitational pull slowly gets weaker as you move up and away from the earth. At a height of 1,600 miles above the earth's surface, for instance, the pull is only half as strong as it is at the surface.

In that case, suppose you throw a ball so hard and make it move upward so fast that by the time it has lost half its speed because of gravitational pull, it is already 1,600 miles up. Even though the ball has only half its original speed, earth's gravity is pulling only half as strongly, and the ball isn't losing speed as fast as it was. The ball keeps moving up more and more slowly, but earth's gravitational pull also gets weaker and weaker.

Under these conditions the ball continues to move upward forever. Though it moves more and more slowly, the weakening gravitational pull can never slow it down all the way. The ball therefore never comes back. The original speed that carries the ball upward so fast that earth's gravity cannot pull it down again is called the *escape velocity*.

The escape velocity on earth is 7 miles per second, or 25,200 miles per hour. If anything is thrown upward at 7 miles per second or faster, it will never come down. It will continue going up forever until it hits something. If it is aimed in the right direction, it will continue going up until it hits the moon.

Here, then, is a way to get to the moon—just have something thrown hard enough.

Of course, no one can throw a ball so hard that it will move 7 miles per second to begin with. There are, however, things more powerful than human muscles.

Gunpowder, for instance, will explode and hurl a cannonball out of a cannon's mouth at speeds much greater than a man can throw. Isn't it possible, then, to have a spaceship with human beings on board shot to the moon?

In 1865 the French science fiction writer Jules Verne wrote a novel called *From the Earth to the Moon*, in which he described a group of men being hurled to the moon by being shot out of a giant cannon.

This sounds good, but there is a catch to it—a deadly catch.

Let us say that the ship is motionless when it is at the bottom of the cannon. An explosive lets go, and the ship comes out of the mouth of the cannon at a speed of at least 7 miles per second. That means the ship increases its speed from nothing at all to 7 miles per second just in the time it takes it to go from the bottom of the cannon to the mouth. Such an increase in speed is called an *acceleration* (*AK-sel-uh-RAY-shun*), from a Latin word meaning "to make quicker."

But if you are in a ship that is speeding up, or accelerating, that ship will push against you to make you speed up, too. It makes you feel as though you are pushing back against it. You can feel this backward push in a car when it accelerates. You can feel a downward push in an elevator when it accelerates upward.

The greater the acceleration, the faster the speed increases and the harder you are pushed back against the seat or downward toward the ground. If a ship were fired by a cannon and went from no movement to 7 miles per second in a very short time, the acceleration would be so great and you would feel yourself pressed back so hard that your body would be crushed and you would be killed.

If a ship were fired out of a cannon as Jules Verne described, every person on board would be killed at once.

AN ILLUSTRATION FROM JULES VERNE'S "VOYAGE FROM THE EARTH TO THE MOON"

Yet we must have that speed. The trick is, then, to accelerate to high speeds, but to do it slowly. How?

The beginning of the answer came from an English scientist, Isaac Newton.

ISAAC NEWTON

3 Rockets

IN 1687 NEWTON wrote a book in which he described how the force of gravitation works. As part of the book he worked out the *three laws of motion*. The third law is this: "For every action in one direction, there is a reaction equal in size in the opposite direction."

Suppose, for instance, that you are sitting on a smooth aluminum platter that is resting on a large, level sheet of very slippery ice. On the platter with you are many heavy metal balls. You pick up one of the balls and throw it in a certain direction. That is the action.

As soon as you throw the ball, the platter starts sliding along the ice in the direction opposite to that in which you threw the ball. That is the reaction. The platter doesn't move as fast as the ball moved because the platter is heavier, or "more massive." The platter's mass times its speed is equal to the ball's mass times its speed. That means the action and reaction are equal.

If you throw another ball in the same direction as the first, the platter gets another kick and begins to move faster. If you throw ball after ball, the platter slides along faster and faster. If you throw enough balls in the same direction, one after another, you can lift the speed of the platter to high levels. If you had enough balls and enough strength, and if the sheet of ice were large enough and slippery enough, you could finally get the platter to go at 7 miles per second. The acceleration would have been so gradual, it wouldn't have hurt you at all.

This has nothing to do with air. If there were no air to get in the way, the platter would speed up more easily. If the platter were in outer space, with nothing but vacuum all about it, then action and reaction would work better than it could on earth.

In 1891 a German inventor, Hermann Ganswindt (*GAN-shvint*), suggested a spaceship that would work by firing balls out of it through a cannon. The acceleration wouldn't hurt anyone on the ship because it would be very gradual, just a small jerk with each firing.

That kind of cannon firing is much more practical than Jules Verne's kind, but only once a ship is already in outer space. Getting a ship from the surface of the earth into outer space is different. Ganswindt's idea wouldn't be practical for that.

If the ship were on earth's surface to begin with and a ball were fired, the earth's gravity would start slowing the ship, so the next ball would have to be fired almost at once in order to avoid having the ship lose too much speed. The balls would have to be fired so rapidly that it is hard to see how to arrange the cannons to work them quickly enough.

HERMANN GANSWINDT'S SPACESHIP

Suppose, instead, we figure out some way of having something fired in one direction in one long spurt. In that way, the ship would move in the other direction in a slow, steady acceleration.

Actually, the right way of doing this was known in Ganswindt's time, and in Jules Verne's time, and even many centuries before. The right way is to make use of something called a *rocket*.

Suppose you have a cardboard cylinder that is closed at one end. You pack it with gunpowder; then you lightly close the open end and leave a fuse passing through. One end of the fuse is in the gunpowder, and the other is out in the open where you can light it. The cylinder is attached to a long thin stick that will steady it when it is moving and keep it going in one direction. This is a *skyrocket* of the kind we fire on the Fourth of July.

Now light the fuse. When the fuse burns down,

SKYROCKET

the fire touches the gunpowder and begins to burn very rapidly, forming large quantities of gases. If the cylinder were tightly closed, the gases would expand and make a loud and damaging explosion. But one end is only loosely closed. The gases come out of that with a hissing noise, and the rocket moves in the opposite direction. The rocket moves faster and faster as the gas "exhaust" keeps on coming out, and it reaches its top speed when all the gunpowder is used up. After that, it slows up and finally falls to the ground.

Gunpowder was invented by the Chinese. In the 1200s the Chinese were making rockets and other fireworks for the fun of watching lights and hearing bangs. They also used rockets in battles to scare the enemy.

Knowledge of gunpowder and rockets spread westward to Europe in the course of the 1200s. Europeans used gunpowder mainly in cannons, but they used rockets only for amusement.

In the 1780s, however, the British were fighting against Indian troops in India. The Indians used rockets to hurl stones against the British. A British officer, William Congreve, who was in charge of the cannons, observed this. It seemed to him that rockets, properly built, could shoot farther and do greater damage than cannons could.

He designed improved rockets, and in the early 1800s the British army and navy used these rockets against their enemies. One of the enemies was the young nation—the United States of America.

Between 1812 and 1814 the United States and Great Britain were at war, and in 1814 the British laid siege to Fort McHenry in the harbor of Baltimore, Maryland. Among other things they fired rockets at the fort.

All night long the bombardment continued, and from one of the British ships an American, Francis Scott Key (who had come to try to rescue another American held prisoner on the ship), watched anxiously. When the dawn came, Key saw the American flag still flying over the fort and knew that the British bombardment had failed. Jubilantly, he wrote a poem that we now know as "The Star-Spangled Banner." It eventually became the American national anthem. At one point in the first stanza, he describes the night bombardment, saying: "*And the rockets' red glare, the bombs bursting in air—*"

Americans still sing about those Congreve rockets. Those rockets weren't used for many years, for cannons continued to be improved, and pretty soon they were firing heavier balls faster and farther than the rockets could.

"AND THE ROCKETS' RED GLARE"

This didn't mean that the rockets weren't ever used again. During World War II, in the early 1940s, rockets were tried once more. As an example of that, soldiers carried tubes called *bazookas*, through which they could fire rockets against tanks.

Also during World War II airplanes were developed that used the rocket principle. The exhaust came out the rear in a great jet of gas, and the plane moved forward faster and faster. In 1952 such *jet planes* began to be used for peaceful purposes. Nowadays many people fly all over the world in jet planes.

Rockets will work in a vacuum even better than in air, so why can't this kind of action and reaction be used to send a ship from the earth to the moon?

The first time this idea was suggested was in 1650. This was nearly 40 years before Newton first presented the world with the idea of action and reaction. The man who made the suggestion was a French science-fiction writer named Cyrano de Bergerac (*sir-ah-NOH-duh-ber-zheh-RAK*).

He wrote a book called *Voyage to the Moon,* and in it he listed seven different ways of reaching the moon. Six of the ways couldn't possibly work, but the seventh was by means of rockets. (Cyrano had a large nose and fought many duels with people who made fun of him. There is a famous play about him, so most people remember his nose and his duels and forget that he was a science fiction writer.)

It was two and a half centuries after that before any scientist discussed rockets as a way of traveling through outer space. The one who did so was a Russian named Konstantin E. Tsiolkovsky *(tsyul-KUV-skee)*. He was born on September 17, 1857. An ear infection when he was only nine years old left him almost entirely deaf, and he didn't have much of a chance to be educated in the Russia of those days.

However, he managed to learn what he needed out of books, and he came up with some very original ideas.

In 1895 he began to write about spaceships. Like Cyrano, Tsiolkovsky thought spaceships should be driven by rockets. Tsiolkovsky didn't think of using gunpowder in the rockets, however. He thought of

KONSTANTIN TSIOLKOVSKY

liquid fuels like kerosene. Such fuels deliver much more driving power than gunpowder does, and because they are liquid, they can be more easily controlled. They can be burned quickly or slowly, depending on how much liquid is pumped to the place where it is being burned.

We use liquid fuels in most of our vehicles today. We use gasoline in automobiles and airplanes, for instance. To deliver the power, though, the gasoline must be combined with the oxygen in the air—a simple matter when vehicles move through air.

It is different, though, for anything moving through the vacuum of space. There is no air around it, and to travel through a vacuum, a rocket must carry its own oxygen, cooled into a liquid so that more oxygen can be squeezed into a small space.

Tsiolkovsky saw that, and in 1903 he began a series of articles for an aviation magazine in which he went into rocketry in considerable detail. Not only did he discuss liquid fuel and liquid oxygen, but he wrote about space suits, the colonizing of space, and so on. In later life he wrote a science fiction novel called *Outside the Earth*.

Although Tsiolkovsky figured out a great deal of the ways in which rockets worked, he never tried to build any. He died on September 19, 1935. Although he was respected in the Soviet Union, hardly anyone outside that country had heard of him.

R. H. GODDARD
1915

4 Liquid-Fuel Rockets

THE FIRST PERSON actually to build a liquid-fuel rocket was an American scientist, Robert Hutchings Goddard. He was born in Worcester, Massachusetts, on October 5, 1882.

As a boy he was interested in science fiction and read H. G. Wells's *The War of the Worlds*. This was published in 1898 and described an invasion of the earth by intelligent beings from Mars.

His reading inspired Goddard to some pretty fanciful ideas of his own. While he was still in college, he wrote an essay called "Traveling in 1950." He described trains pulled along by magnets through tunnels from which all the air had been removed. He imagined such trains going from Boston to New York in ten minutes. (Unfortunately, when 1950 came there were no such trains, and the trip still took four hours, as it does even today.)

Then Goddard grew interested in rockets. By 1914 he had already obtained two patents for inventions involving rockets. In 1919 he put out a small book, only 69 pages long, that described rockets and how they might be used to reach the moon. He had very much the same ideas that Tsiolkovsky had had.

Goddard then went on to build rockets that used gasoline and liquid oxygen. On March 16, 1926, on his aunt's farm in Auburn, Massachusetts, he was ready to send up the first such rocket. His wife took a picture of him and his rocket. It was a cold day, and there was snow on the ground. Goddard, wearing overcoat and boots, was standing next to what looked like a jungle gym. At the top of it was a small rocket, four feet long and six inches thick.

There were no reporters watching. In fact, there was no one watching, for no one was interested. Yet Goddard was the Columbus of space flight. He was about to fire the first rocket of the kind that would eventually go out into space.

Goddard lit the fuse, and the rocket rose 184 feet into the air, reaching a speed of 60 miles an hour. That wasn't much, but it showed that Goddard's rocket engine worked. Now he had to build bigger rockets.

Goddard managed to get a few thousand dollars from the Smithsonian Institution in Washington, and in July 1929, he sent up a larger rocket near Worcester, Massachusetts. It went faster and higher than the first. It also carried a barometer, a thermometer, and a small camera. It was the first rocket to carry instruments of the kind that might test what it is like in the upper air or in outer space.

But Goddard was having trouble. People thought he was peculiar, and they laughed at him when they

R. H. GODDARD'S FIRST LIQUID FUELED ROCKET

found out he thought human beings could reach the moon. *The New York Times* printed an editorial saying that Goddard was foolish, since his rockets wouldn't work in outer space where there was no air. All that editorial showed was that the person writing it was ignorant and did not understand action and reaction.

Then one of Goddard's rockets made a loud noise when being launched. The neighbors called firemen and policemen, and Goddard was ordered to stop all his rocket experiments.

Fortunately, the aviator Charles Lindbergh heard of the experiments, and he used his influence to get Goddard $50,000. Goddard used the money to build himself a place in New Mexico where he could continue his experiments. It was a lonely place where the noise of his rockets would bother nobody.

Here he built larger rockets and worked out almost all the inventions that were to be used in rockets in years to come.

For instance, he invented the use of rockets in more than one stage. The bottom part of such a rocket, the first stage, is full of fuel and oxygen that burns and lifts the rocket high in the air. When the burning is finished, that heavy first stage of the rocket falls off, and the part above it, the second stage, starts combining the fuel and oxygen *it* contains.

The burning in the second stage drives the rocket higher still and makes it go faster, all the more so since it is not being dragged down by the heavy first stage, which has dropped off. When the second stage is finished, it drops off, and a third stage carries on.

TWO-STAGE ROCKET

In this way, a rocket can go higher and faster than it could if all the fuel and oxygen were carried in one big stage.

Before Goddard was finished, he had 214 patents in rocketry. Between 1930 and 1935, he launched rockets that got up to the speed of 550 miles an hour and reached a height of a mile and a half.

For the most part, though, there continued to be almost no interest in Goddard's work. Nobody even seemed to know that there was anything going on. Certainly, the American government did nothing at all to encourage him.

Things were different in Germany. There, interest in rocketry started with a book put out in 1923 by Hermann Oberth (*OH-bert*), a Rumanian of German descent. His ideas were similar to those already expressed by Tsiolkovsky and Goddard.

In 1927 the "Society for Space Travel" was started

WERNER VON BRAUN

in Germany. One of the first members was a young man named Willy Ley, who then introduced another young man, Werner von Braun, to the Society.

The Society built and fired liquid-fuel rockets, launching 85 of them. One of them reached a height of nearly a mile. The Society didn't do quite as well as Goddard was doing working all by himself, but it began to get important help.

In 1933 Adolf Hitler became ruler of Germany. He was a harsh and cruel man who intended to make Germany very powerful and then go to war in order to take over as many neighboring nations as he could. He decided that rockets would make a good war weapon, so he backed the work of the Society.

Willy Ley was horrified at Hitler's beliefs and left Germany at once. Werner von Braun stayed behind, though, and headed the rocket work for Hitler.

In 1936 a secret place for rocket experiments was built on the shores of the Baltic Sea in northeastern Germany. With plenty of government money Werner von Braun began to make progress. By 1938 he was building rockets that could fly eleven miles.

The next year World War II began in Europe, and it was Hitler's idea to have von Braun develop *missiles*—rockets that could carry explosives and that could be accurately aimed at places hundreds of miles away in enemy territory. They would move so quickly that airplanes and antiaircraft guns wouldn't be able to shoot them down.

The first weapon of this sort was a kind of automatic plane called *V-1*. The *V* stood for *Vergeltung* which was the German word for "vengeance." By 1944, though, von Braun had ready a much better missile that was a true rocket and would go faster than the speed of sound. It was the *V-2 rocket*.

Altogether, 4,300 V-2 rockets were fired by the Germans, and 1,230 of them hit London. The missiles killed 2,511 Englishmen and seriously wounded 5,869 others. Luckily for the world, the V-2 rocket came too late to save Hitler. He was already losing

V-2 ROCKET

the war when the rockets started to fly, and they weren't enough to turn back the armies that were closing in on him. Germany surrendered on May 8, 1945.

Goddard lived long enough to see the V-2 rockets in action. He died on August 10, 1945.

One thing the V-2 rockets did was to get both the United States and the Soviet Union (the two big winners of World War II) interested in rockets. After all, each of these nations feared the other and therefore needed all the weapons it could get. Each nation therefore tried to capture German rocket experts when their armies moved into Germany. The United States got von Braun himself.

Both nations then worked hard to build bigger and better missiles. By the 1950s the old V-2 was just a toy compared to the monster missiles being built. Eventually, both the United States and the Soviet

Union had missiles that could be aimed at and made to hit any place on earth. What's more, the missiles wouldn't carry ordinary explosives as the V-2s had; they would carry atomic bombs.

Both nations now had weapons that could destroy each other and perhaps most of the rest of the world. Certainly nothing like that had been in the minds of Tsiolkovsky and Goddard. They had wanted the rockets for the exploration of outer space.

That was happening, too. The United States, when it invaded Germany, had captured a number of the V-2 rockets, which they used for scientific purposes. They did not send them against cities, but straight up in the air. The V-2s did not carry explosives, but instruments to record various properties of the upper air. One of these V-2s reached a height of 114 miles, four times the height any balloon or plane could reach.

In 1949 the United States put a small American rocket on top of a V-2. When the V-2 had reached its maximum height, the small rocket took off and reached a height of 240 miles. When heights of over a hundred miles are reached, the rockets are practically in outer space.

Still, any rocket that goes shooting high up in the air and is then pulled down by earth's gravity stays in outer space only for a few minutes. That isn't nearly enough time to study the properties of outer space in detail.

Is there any way to keep a rocket in outer space for a long time without having it fall back to earth?

Yes, there is, and in the 1950s both the United States and the Soviet Union began to think about that.

SPUTNIK

5 Satellites and Spaceships

SUPPOSE A ROCKET is fired a hundred miles or more upward and is then sent sideways so that it goes along parallel to the earth's surface. The rocket begins to fall downward, but the earth's surface is round and curves away from the rocket.

If the rocket moves at a fast enough speed, it falls downward at the same speed that the earth's surface curves away. In that case the rocket does not reach the ground. It just goes round and round the earth. It is *in orbit* around the earth. Such a rocket is called a *satellite*. The moon is a natural satellite of the earth. A rocket in orbit is an artificial satellite.

Nearly 300 years ago, Isaac Newton showed that artificial satellites are possible. To put one in orbit, however, is a matter of speed. A satellite has to travel at least 5 miles per second if it is to stay in orbit about 100 miles above the earth's surface.

It wasn't till the 1950s that the United States and the Soviet Union had rockets that were powerful enough to produce such speeds. In 1955 the United

States announced it was going to try to put a satellite into orbit. The Soviet Union announced it would try to do the same thing.

Most Americans were certain that the United States would manage to do it first, but they were surprised. On October 4, 1957, the Soviet Union put into orbit the first artificial satellite ever launched. They had meant to launch it in time to serve as a celebration of the hundredth anniversary of Tsiolkovsky's birth on September 17, but it had been delayed. October 4, 1957, is often considered the beginning of the "space age."

The United States was soon launching satellites of its own. On January 31, 1958, von Braun managed to put the first American satellite into orbit. In the years that followed, hundreds of satellites have been launched by each nation.

These satellites study conditions on earth. There are satellites that take pictures of the earth from outer space. In that way, scientists can study the cloud patterns and can better understand the weather. Hurricanes can be seen from the beginning and can be followed.

There are satellites that can receive messages from one point on the earth and relay them to another. In this way it has become possible for people in a particular place on earth to see any other place by TV.

The way a satellite moves in orbit can be used to study the gravitational pull of earth at different places. The exact shape of the earth can be studied in this way. The earth can be mapped more accurately, too.

ADVANCED SATELLITES

EXPLORER XVII

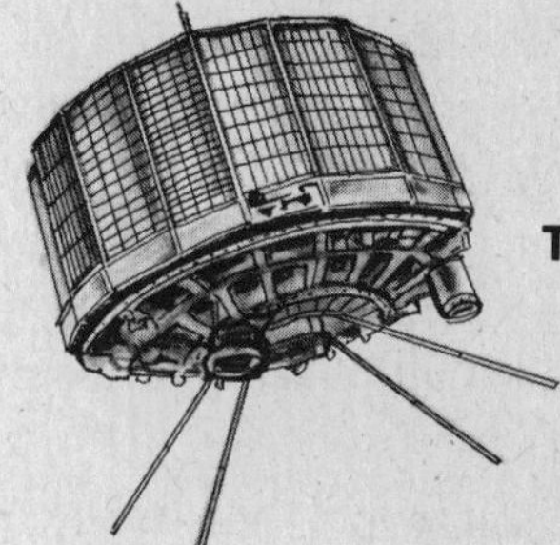
TIROS I

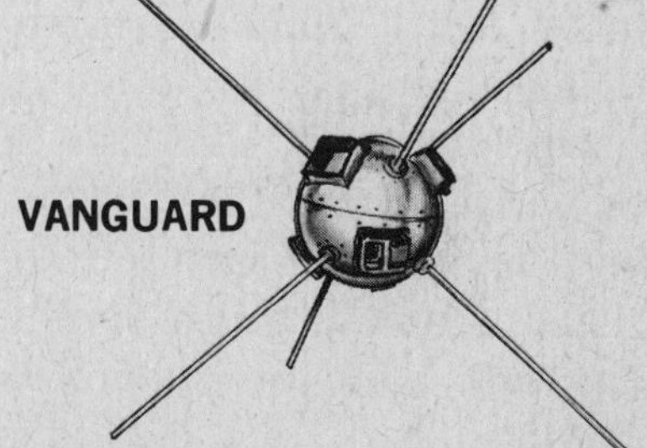
VANGUARD

TELSTAR

Some satellites study radiation from the sky that cannot pass through earth's layer of air. The satellites study it before it reaches the air. They study radiation from the sun and from other parts of the sky. New information about space has come in floods, and scientists have learned more about the universe than they possibly could have learned without satellites.

Some satellites, for instance, studied the electrically charged atom fragments above the atmosphere. They found large belts of them around the earth. These belts—called *Van Allen radiation belts*—stretched away from the earth on the side opposite the sun like a long tail. Scientists were completely surprised. They had never suspected such a thing might exist.

If a satellite can be made to go a little faster, it will move away from the earth altogether. Remember that 7 miles per second is escape velocity.

On January 2, 1959, the Soviet Union fired a particularly fast satellite that passed close to the moon and never came back. It went into orbit about the sun. It studied the properties of space near the moon and sent back information by radio. It was the first "probe."

On September 12, 1959, the Soviets aimed another probe so accurately that it hit the moon. It was the first piece of human-made material ever to rest on the surface of another world.

In October 1959 the Soviets sent a probe with cameras around the moon. It sent back the first pictures ever taken of the moon's far side. The moon always shows the same face to the earth, and the far side had never before been seen by human beings.

After that the United States began to send up probes also. Some of the probes went into orbit around the moon so that every spot on the moon was mapped in detail.

Probes were made to land on the moon softly, without being destroyed. There they could take pictures of the moon's surface from close up and analyze the chemical makeup of the surface. Both the Americans and the Soviets did these things, but the Americans got better and more detailed results.

Other probes went farther afield. American probes carried their instruments past Venus and discovered that that planet is much hotter than had been thought. Other American probes traveled to Mars and to Mercury and took close-up photographs that made it possible to prepare detailed maps of those worlds.

Mercury looks very much like the moon. Although Mars also has areas that are full of moonlike craters, some of the Martian surface contains volcanoes and canyons. There are also markings that look like dry river beds.

Still other American probes shot past the distant giant planet Jupiter, and new knowledge about it was obtained. One of those rockets is moving on toward the still more distant planet Saturn.

The Soviets have not had as much success with their probes as the United States has had. However, several Soviet probes have landed on Venus itself and have recorded temperatures and air pressures on its surface.

But could *human beings* be put into orbit? Could

VIKING PHOTO OF THE SURFACE OF MARS

they be sent into space? After all, for thousands of years fiction writers have imagined human beings traveling through space. Was it possible?

There seemed no reason why it couldn't be done. Both the United States and the Soviet Union experimented by launching animals. The very second Soviet satellite, launched on November 3, 1957, carried a live dog. The dog survived the launch and lived until it was painlessly poisoned. There was no way of bringing it back to earth, however.

Later, animals were launched and brought back safely. The United States successfully placed a chimpanzee into orbit and brought it safely back. Both nations began to train men for trips into space. In the United States these men are called *astronauts*; in the Soviet Union they are called *cosmonauts*.

The Soviet Union was the first to put a man into orbit. On April 12, 1961, the Soviet cosmonaut Yuri Gagarin was put in orbit, sent once around the world, and brought back safely. He was the first human being in space. (Seven years later, he died in an airplane crash.)

The first American in space was John H. Glenn, who was launched on February 20, 1962. He went around the world three times before being brought safely down.

In the years that followed, both the United States and the Soviet Union put more and more elaborate man-carrying satellites into orbit. There were satellites that carried two men and even three men. A Soviet satellite launched on June 16, 1963, carried a woman.

Human beings remained in space longer and longer. At first they only remained for hours, then days, then weeks. In 1975 three American astronauts rocketed up to a large space station called *Skylab*, which was in orbit around the earth. They boarded it and remained on it for three *months*. Then they came safely back to earth.

During the 1960s the satellites became more and more like rocketships. They weren't simply put into orbit. They could be maneuvered by the men

YURI GAGARIN
FIRST MAN IN SPACE

JOHN GLENN
FIRST AMERICAN IN SPACE

aboard. Two satellites could join each other, and men could travel from one to the other. Men could put on space suits, leave the ship for a *space walk*, and return.

The Americans began to take a longer and longer lead over the Soviet Union in such experiments. They began to plan to reach the moon before 1970, making use of *Apollo* rockets.

The attempt did not proceed without tragedy. On January 27, 1967, three American astronauts died in a fire while testing an Apollo capsule on the ground.

The effort to reach the Moon was delayed while rocket designs were changed to limit the danger of fire.

The Soviets had tragedy, too. In April 1967, a Soviet cosmonaut died while his rocket ship was returning to Earth.

But the American effort was not stopped. In December 1968 an Apollo rocket ship went out to the moon, circled it ten times at a height of about 70 miles above its surface, then returned safely to earth.

Other close approaches were made, and then the rocket ship *Apollo 11* was sent out to the moon in July 1969 with three men aboard. One man stayed in orbit around the moon, while the other two went down to the surface with part of the ship. On July 20, 1969, Neil Armstrong became the first human being ever to set his foot on the surface of another world. As his foot moved down to touch the moon, he said, "That's one small step for a man, one giant leap for mankind."

Since that great day, five other Apollo ships have landed on the moon. Each has stayed on the moon longer than the ones before, exploring and performing experiments. Then each ship has returned with its crew safely to earth, bringing moon rocks with it.

The Soviet Union has not yet landed men on the moon, but they have sent automatic devices that have brought back some moon material. They have also sent automatic cars to the moon, which have driven about for weeks and sent back information.

After the last Apollo flight was ended in December 1972, interest in the moon seemed to grow less in the

NEIL ARMSTRONG STEPS ONTO THE MOON

United States. There are no plans to send anyone else to the moon, though other kinds of space exploration continue.

Does that mean that humans will no longer go into space?

Perhaps not. Gerard P. O'Neill of Princeton suggested in 1974 that human beings might build space colonies. They could establish a mining station on the moon and use material from the moon to build glass and metal cylinders, spheres, or doughnut-shaped objects in the moon's orbit. Thousands, or even millions, of human beings might live in such colonies.

The people in the colonies could build large devices that would gather energy from the sun and beam it down to earth. In this way, the earth might be able to get along even though all the oil and coal is used up.

Will we do this? Some people don't think so. They think that the notion of building space colonies and of living in them is too fantastic to believe.

But then, not so long ago, people thought that the notion of reaching the moon and walking on its surface was too fantastic to believe.

Perhaps humanity's adventures in space are only beginning.

PROJECTED ORBITING SPACE STATION

Index

Acceleration, 25
Air, 19-22
Airplanes, 16
Aluminum, 14
Apollo *11*, 57
Apollo rockets, 56
Armstrong, Neil, 57
Astronauts, 55

Balloons, 14, 16
Barometer, 20
Bazookas, 34
Braun, Werner von, 44-46, 50

Charles, Jacques, 14
Congreve, William, 33
Cosmonauts, 55
Cyrano de Bergerac, 35

Daedalus, 11
Dirigible, 14

Escape velocity, 24

Flying, 9, 11
Fort McHenry, 33
From the Earth to the Moon, 24

Gagarin, Yuri, 55
Ganswindt, Hermann, 30
Gasoline, 36
Glenn, John H., 55
Gliders, 16
Goddard, Robert Hutchings, 39-43
Godwin, Francis, 12
Gravitation, 23, 24
Gunpowder, 25, 31, 32

Helium, 15
Hitler, Adolf, 45
Hydrogen, 14

Icarus, 11

Jet planes, 34
Jupiter, 53

Kerosene, 36
Key, Francis Scott, 33
Kites, 15

Ley, Willy, 44, 45
Lindbergh, Charles A., 16, 42

Man in the Moone, 12
Mars, 53
Mass, 29
Mercury, 53
Montgolfier, Joseph and
Jacques, 12
Moon, 21, 22
man on the, 57
probes and, 52-53
Moon rocks, 57
Motion, laws of, 29

Newton, Isaac, 27, 29
New York Times, The, 41

Oberth, Hermann, 43
O'Neill, Gerard P., 59
Outer space, 22
Outside the Earth, 37
Oxygen, 19
liquid, 37

Probe, space, 52ff.

Rockets, 31
Apollo, 56
Goddard's, 40
orbiting, 49
stages of, 42
V-2, 45-47
war use of, 33

Satellites, 49ff.
Saturn, 53
Skylab, 55
Skyrocket, 31
Space age, 50
Space colonies, 59
Space, men in, 54ff.
Spacewalk, 56
Star-Spangled Banner, The, 33

Torricelli, Evangelista, 20
Traveling in 1950, 39
Tsiolkovsky, Konstantin E., 35

V-1, 45
V-2 rocket, 45-47
Vacuum, 22
Van Allen radiation belts, 51
Venus, 53
Verne, Jules, 24-25
Voyage to the Moon, 35

War of the Worlds, The, 39
Wells, H. G., 39
Wright, Orville and Wilbur, 16

Zeppelin, Ferdinand von, 14

R. Gupta's®

POPULAR

Translation *for* Schools

by

H.S. BHATIA

M.A. (English)

Formerly Sr. Lecturer in English

(Reader's Grade)

A.S. College, Khanna (Punjab)

RAMESH PUBLISHING HOUSE, NEW DELHI

Published by
O.P. Gupta *for* Ramesh Publishing House

Admin. Office
12-H, New Daryaganj Road, Opp. Officers' Mess,
New Delhi-110002 ✆ 23275224, 23245124

E-mail: info@rameshpublishinghouse.com
For Online Shopping: www.rameshpublishinghouse.com

Showroom
- Balaji Market, Nai Sarak, Delhi-6 ✆ 23253720, 23282525
- 4457, Nai Sarak, Delhi-6, ✆ 23918938

Book Code: R-219

15th Edition: November, 2023

ISBN: 978-81-7812-522-0

Price: ₹ 85

Printed at: Shyam Printer, Delhi